Sarah Quartel Songbook

10 songs for mixed voices

MUSIC DEPARTMENT

OXFORD
UNIVERSITY PRESS

OXFORD
UNIVERSITY PRESS

Great Clarendon Street, Oxford OX2 6DP,
United Kingdom

Oxford University Press is a department of the University of Oxford.
It furthers the University's objective of excellence in research, scholarship,
and education by publishing worldwide. Oxford is a registered trade mark of
Oxford University Press in the UK and in certain other countries

ISBN 978–0–19–355104–6

Music and text origination by Katie Johnston
Printed in Great Britain on acid-free paper by
Halstan & Co. Ltd, Amersham, Bucks.

Contents

Introduction

It is such a pleasure to see these pieces together in one collection. We begin with 'Wide Open Spaces', which received its premiere under the baton of Bob Chilcott at the American Choral Directors Association National Conference in 2014. A year later, Bob included 'I know a bank where the wild thyme blows' in his edited collection of Shakespeare settings, *Shall I compare thee?*. I would not be where I am today without his tremendous support, mentorship, and advocacy!

A choir of nearly 500 singers premiered 'Sing, my Child' at the 2016 International Choral Kathaumixw in British Columbia and, in 2018, the SATB version of 'Voice on the Wind' was premiered by Gemischter Chor ANGUSTA of Japan. "Hope' is the thing with feathers' was written for Ely Consort in England, and this mixed-voice version of 'All the way home' was commissioned by Penn High School in Indiana.

This arrangement of 'How can I keep from singing?' was completed when I was pregnant with my son in 2017 and was the first piece I sang to him after he was born. 'Swept Away' also holds a special place in my heart, as it was written for my husband while he was deployed with the Royal Canadian Navy. 'The Parting Glass' is dedicated to a friend as a welcome home from his own deployment with the Canadian Armed Forces.

Although published here for the first time, 'One of these Days' may be the oldest song in this collection. It was originally written for a sensational Finnish pop singer and has found new life in this six-part *a cappella* arrangement.

As I look at the titles included in this collection and remember the people who have inspired them, I am reminded that choral music-making holds a tremendous power to connect and unite us. I am thankful to every person who inspired these pieces and grateful to Robyn Elton and Laura Jones for bringing this collection to life.

Sarah Quartel
March 2021

*Commissioned by the American Choral Directors Association
for the Middle School/Junior High School Boys' Honor Choir, Bob Chilcott conductor,
Salt Lake City, Utah, February 28, 2014.
Sponsored by Classical Movements, Inc.*

Wide Open Spaces

Words and music by
SARAH QUARTEL
(b. 1982)

Duration: 3 mins

Also available in versions for TTBB and piano (ISBN 978-0-19-341339-9) and SSAA and piano (ISBN 978-0-19-355096-4).

There's part of my jour-ney_____ that's yet to be

found._____ With life all a-round us_____

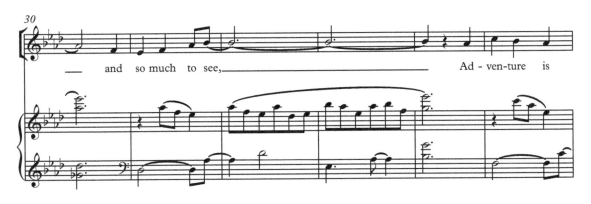

_ and so much to see,_____ Ad-ven-ture is

call-ing,_____ It's call-ing to me._____

Out in the wide o - pen spa - ces a - round me.

S./A.

T./B. TENORS & BASSES *unis.* **mf**

With big sky a - bove

T./B.

— me, I'm on my way,

sim.

— Scan-ning the ho - ri - zon of a brand new day.

Feet to the earth___ now,___

___ there's no turn-ing back.___ In - to the world___

___ now,___ look at me, look at me go!

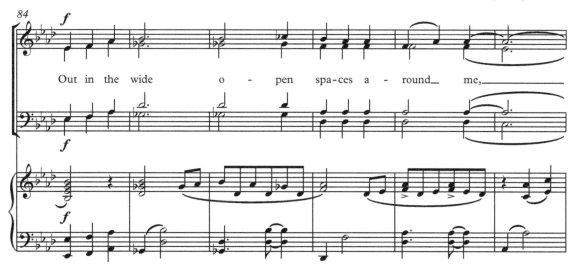

Out in the wide o - pen spa-ces a - round_ me,_____

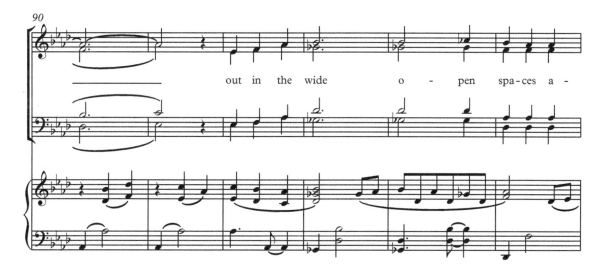

_____ out in the wide o - pen spa-ces a -

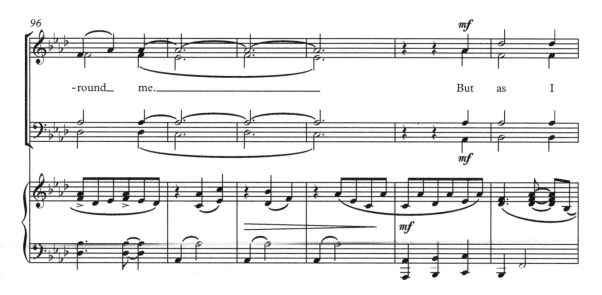

-round_ me._____ But as I

jour - ney out_____ I look_____ with - in and

see____ The spa-ces in-side____ of____ me_____ yet to____

— be filled, Filled_ with what I have seen_____

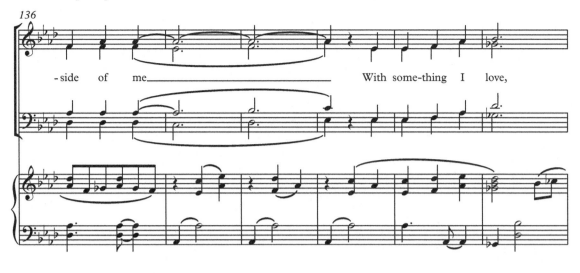

136

-side of me_____ With some-thing I love,

142

some - thing I___ would like to be, be,___ be!

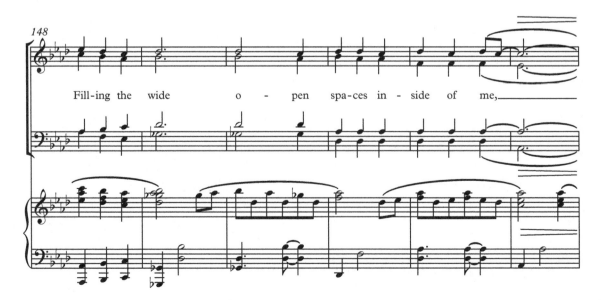

148

Fill-ing the wide o - pen spa-ces in - side of me,_____

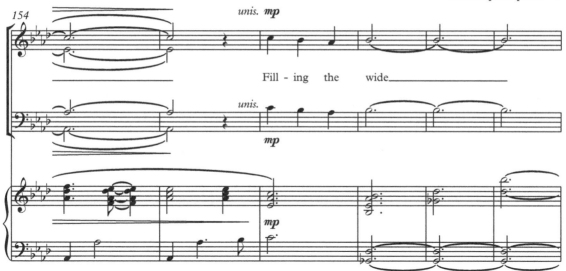

Fill - ing the wide_____

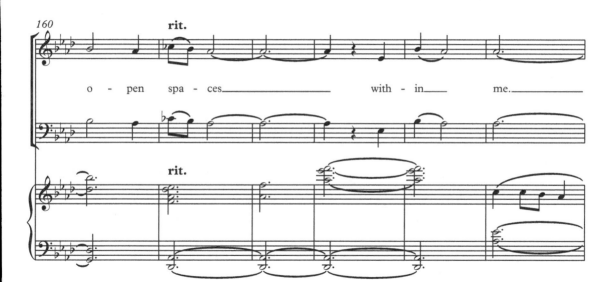

o - pen spa - ces_____ with - in____ me.____

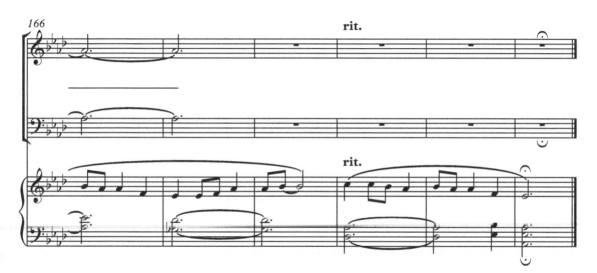

Commissioned for the 2016 International Choral Kathaumixw
Paul Cummings, Artistic Director

Sing, my Child

Words and music by
SARAH QUARTEL

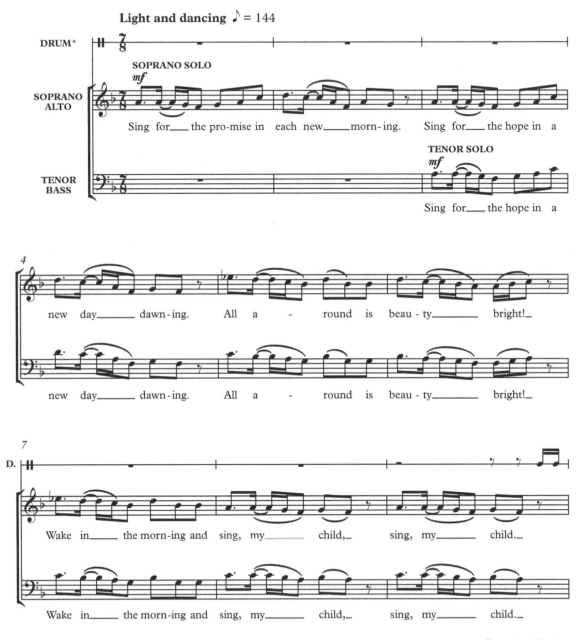

Duration: 4.5 mins

* A cajón or large djembe is preferred, but any hand drum with a deep, rich sound will work well.

Also available in a version for SSAA and hand drum (ISBN 978–0–19–353024–9).

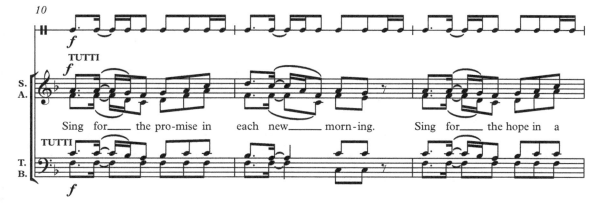

Sing for____ the pro-mise in   each new____ morn-ing.   Sing for____ the hope in a

new day____ dawn-ing.   All a - round is beau-ty____ bright!_

Wake in____ the morn-ing and   sing, my____ child,   sing, my____ child,

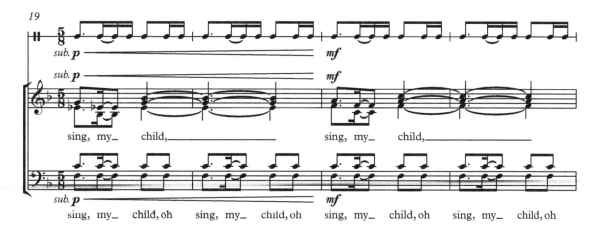

sing, my_ child,____   sing, my_ child,____

sing, my_ child, oh   sing, my_ child, oh   sing, my_ child, oh   sing, my_ child, oh

sing, my__ child.

ah

sing, my__ child, oh   sing, my__ child, oh   sing, my__ child, oh   sing, my__ child.

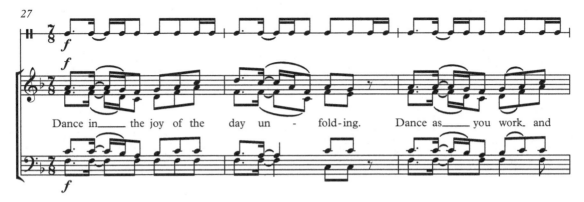

Dance in____ the joy of the   day un - fold-ing.   Dance as____ you work and

dance as____ you're learn-ing.   All a - round is beau-ty____ bright!_

Take in____ the day__ and   dance, my_____ child,_   dance, my_____ child,_

poco rit.

dance, my_____ child,_____ dance, my_____ child._____

Strong, like a hymn ♩ = 96

But__ when trou - bles come and wor - ry is

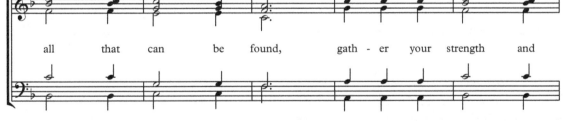

all that can be found, gath - er your strength and

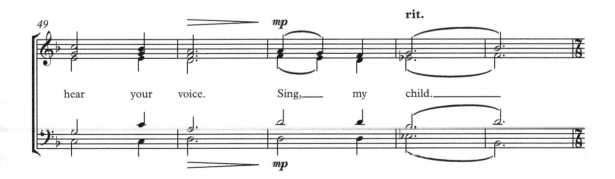

hear your voice. Sing,___ my child._____

Tempo I ♪ = 144

Laugh in___ the cool and the fresh of___ the ev'n-ing. Laugh in___ your tri - umph,

Laugh, laugh, oh laugh, my child, laugh, laugh, oh laugh, my child, laugh, laugh, oh laugh, my child,

laugh in___ suc-ceed-ing. All a - round_ is beau-ty___ bright!

laugh, laugh, oh laugh, my child, laugh, laugh, oh laugh, my child, laugh, laugh, oh laugh, my child,

Peace in___ the still-ness and

Rest in___ the ev'n-ing and laugh, my___ child. Peace,___

laugh, laugh, oh laugh, my child, laugh, laugh, my child.

dark of___ the night. Peace in___ the dreams of your si - lent___ de - lights.

peace,___ peace,___ peace,___

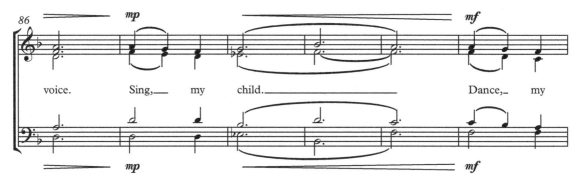

voice.   Sing,— my   child._____   Dance,— my

child._____   Laugh,— my   child._____

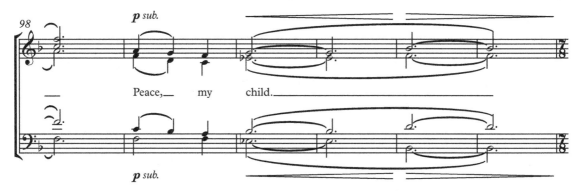

Peace,— my   child._____

♩ = ♪   **rit.**

SOPRANO AND TENOR SOLO

Peace, my_____   child,— oh,   peace, my_____   child._____

*oo*_____   *oo*

In memory of Kassidy
Commissioned by Viva Voce of Penn High School Choir, Mishawaka, IN
Andrew Nemeth, Director

All the way home

Text written and inspired by
members of the Radcliffe Ladies' Choir as they
reflected on their motto, "friendship through singing"

SARAH QUARTEL

Duration: 3.5 mins

Also available in versions for SSA and piano (ISBN 978–0–19–352590–0) and solo voice and piano (high voice ISBN 978–0–19–354742–1)/
low voice ISBN 978–0–19–354743–8).

joy-ful, with har-mon-ies sing me all the way
-long,

home with a song in my heart. All the way home

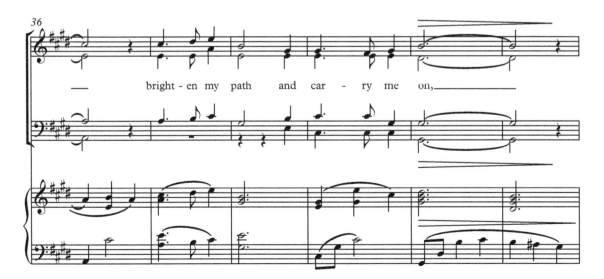

bright-en my path and car-ry me on,

all_____ the way home._____

There's a beau - ti - ful pow'r in what____ we bring,_____ there's

strength in the glor - ious song____ we sing._____ Eas - ing all

trou - bles, calm-ing all fears,_____ joy - ful, with har - mon-ies sing

me   all   the way home with a song in my heart.   All_____ the way

home_____   bright-en my path and car - ry me on,_____

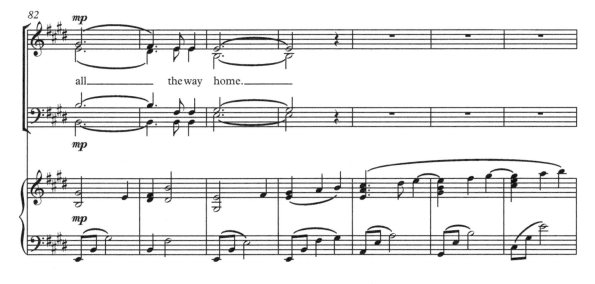

all____ the way home.____

poco meno mosso

ah____

poco meno mosso

T./B.

Eve - ning brings a shin - ing star,____ her an - cient an - thems__

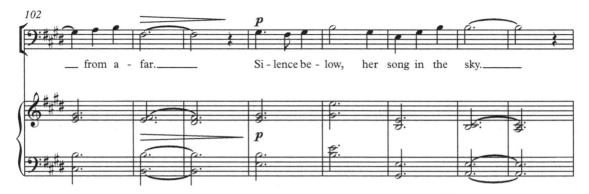

__ from a - far._____ Si - lence be - low,   her song in the   sky._____

S./A.

Joy - ful with har - mon - ies   sing   me_____ all   the way_ home   with a

T./B.

song   in   my heart.   All_____   the way   home_____

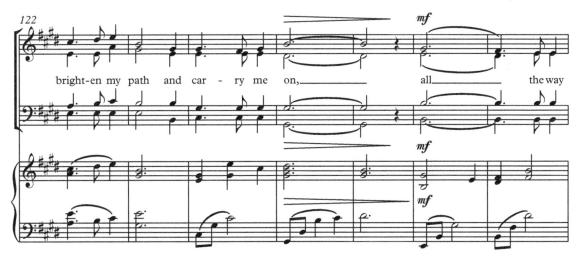

bright-en my path and car - ry me on,_____ all_____ the way

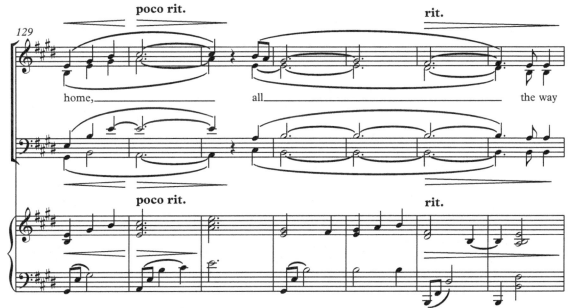

home,_____ all_____ the way

home._____

How can I keep from singing?

Text unattributed (adapted)

ROBERT LOWRY (1826–99)
arr. SARAH QUARTEL

Duration: 4 mins

Also available in a version for SSAA unaccompanied (ISBN 978–0–19–352208–4).

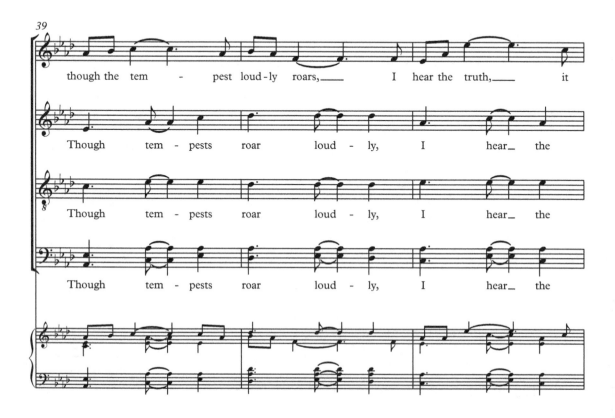

42

45

* *close*, the verb, with a 'z' sound

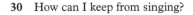

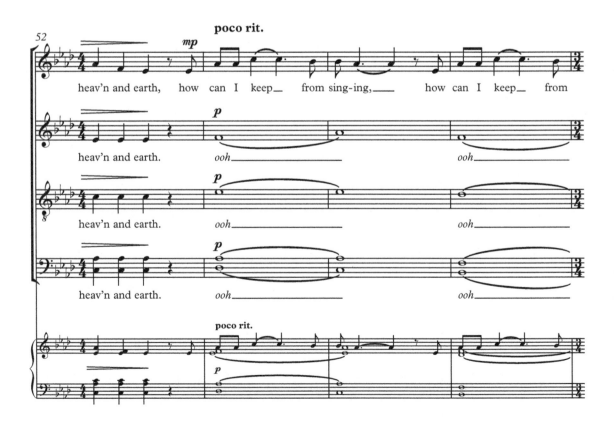

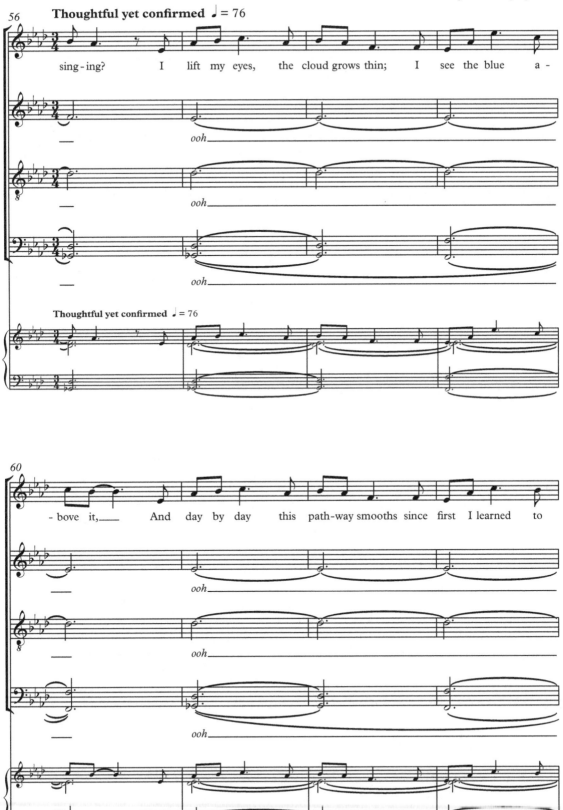

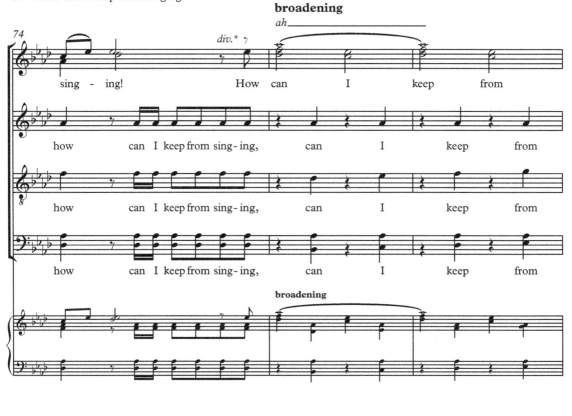

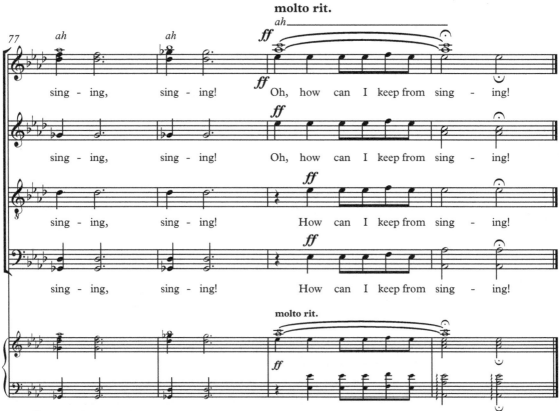

* small notes solo (optional)

for Ely Consort

'Hope' is the thing with feathers

Emily Dickinson (1830–86)

SARAH QUARTEL

Duration: 3.5 mins

for the sailor I love

Swept Away

Words and music by
SARAH QUARTEL

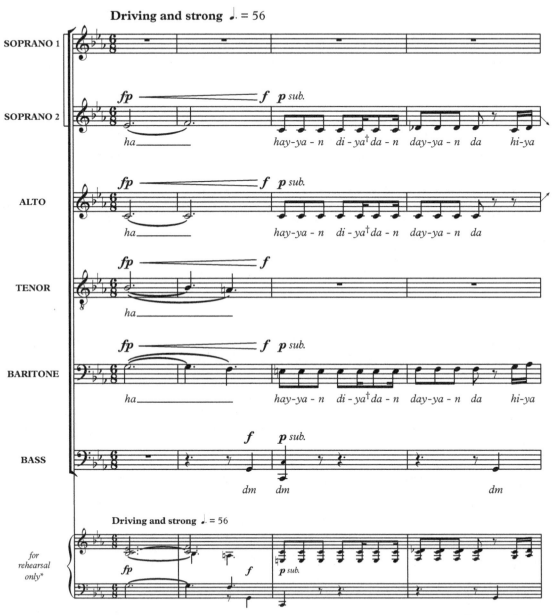

Duration: 4 mins

† pronounced 'dye-ya'

* The piano reduction includes the rhythmic accompanying parts throughout; for reasons of playability, melodic lines are sometimes omitted.

* The vowel sound for 'hae' and 'yae' should be 'a' as in 'cat', with North American pronunciation.

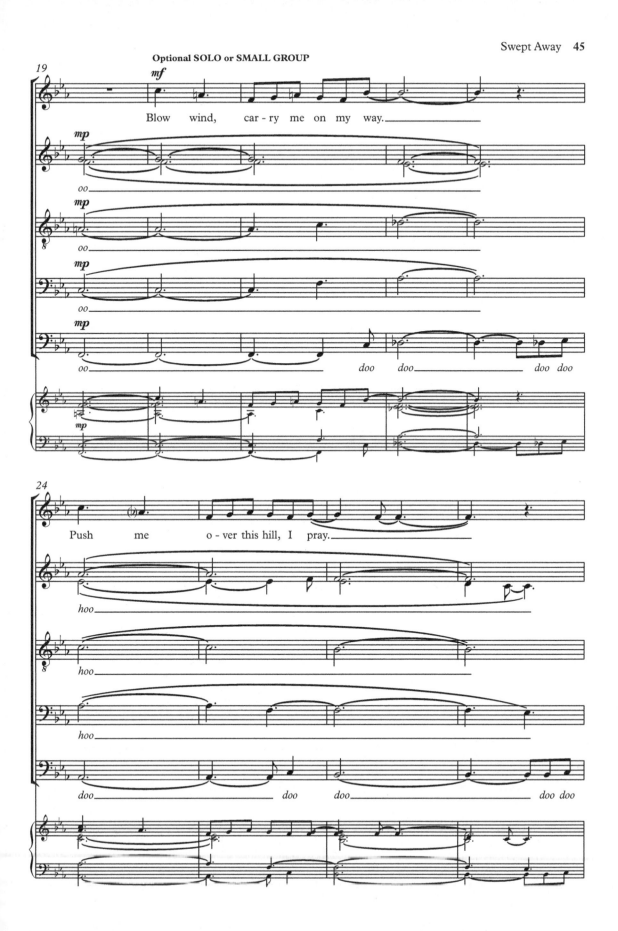

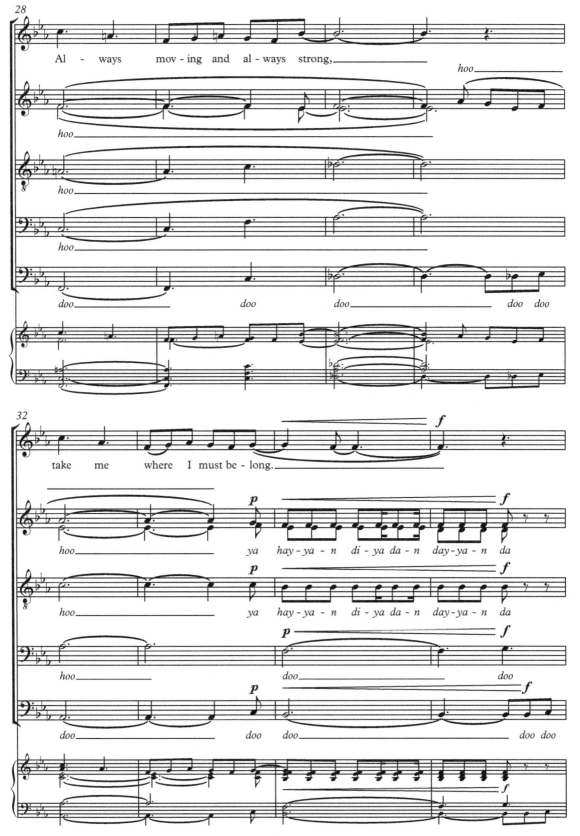

*Commissioned by Gemischter Chor ANGUSTA, Sapporo City, Japan,
and their artistic director Takayuki Fukuda*

Voice on the Wind

Words and music by
SARAH QUARTEL

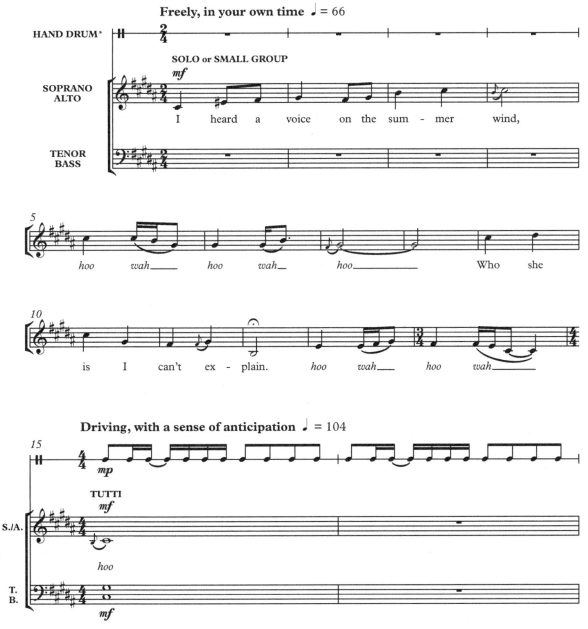

Duration: 4 mins

* Alternatively a bodhrán may be used.

Also available in a version for SSAA and hand drum (ISBN 978–0–19–341013–8).

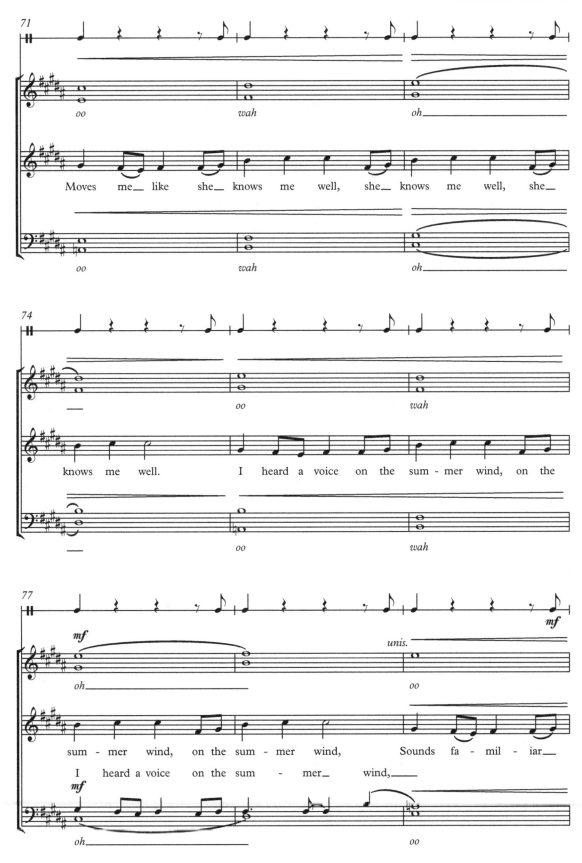

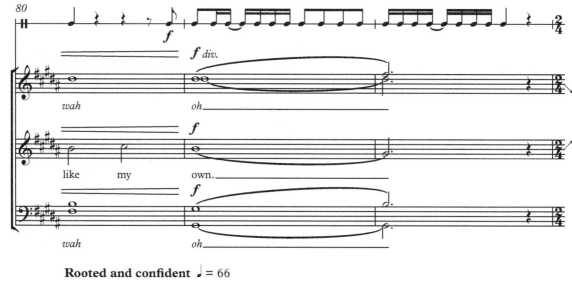

Rooted and confident ♩ = 66

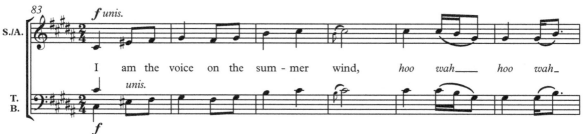

I am the voice on the sum - mer wind, hoo wah___ hoo wah_

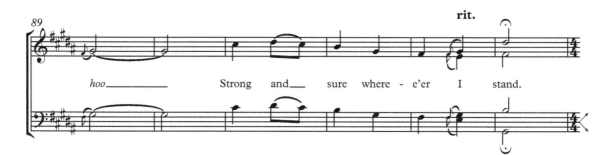

hoo___ Strong and___ sure where - e'er I stand.

Strong and driving to the end ♩ = 104

hoo wah hoo wah hoo wah hoo hoo wah___ ya

hoo wah hoo wah hoo wah hoo hoo wah hoo wah hoo wah hoo

hoo wah hoo wah hoo wah hoo hoo wah___ ya

Commissioned by the Agincourt Singers (James Pinhorn, Conductor)
in celebration of the one hundredth anniversary of the Agincourt Collegiate Institute

I know a bank where the wild thyme blows

William Shakespeare
from *A Midsummer Night's Dream* (Act 2, Scene 1)

SARAH QUARTEL

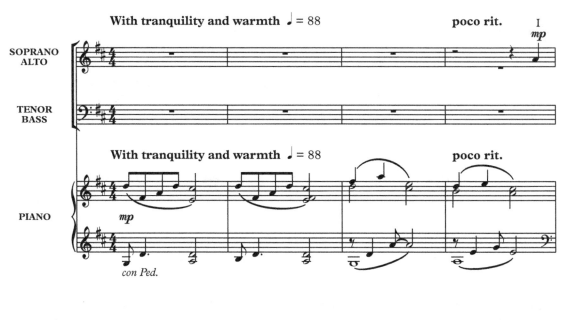

Duration: 3.5 mins

Originally published in *Shall I compare thee?* (ISBN 978–0–19–340614–8).

* *eglantine* = sweet briar, a species of wild rose

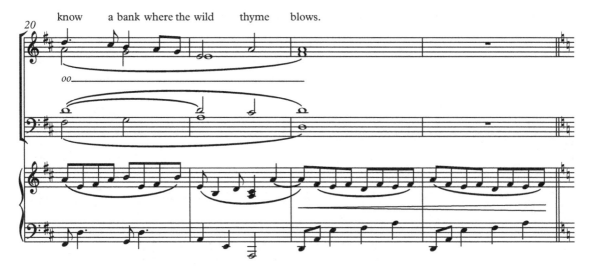

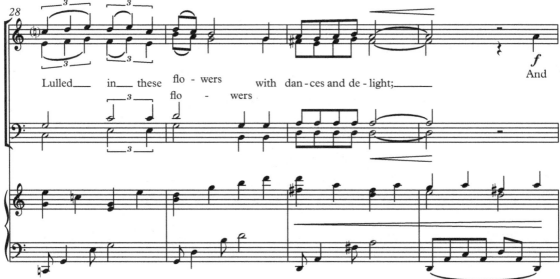

* *throws* = sheds, † *weed* = garments

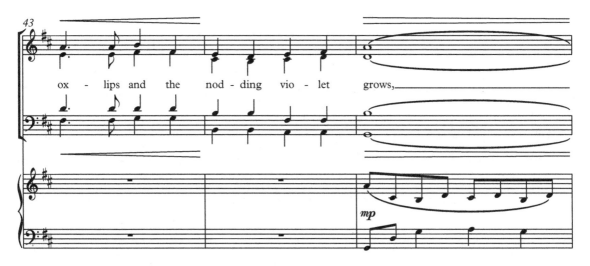

ox - lips and the nod - ding vio - let grows,

Quite o - ver - can - o - pied___ with lus - cious

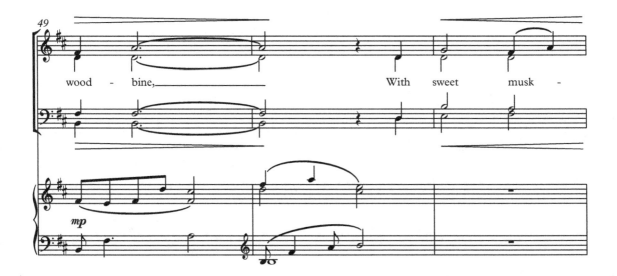

wood - bine,___ With sweet musk -

One of these Days

Words and music by
SARAH QUARTEL

Duration: 4 mins

* The piano reduction includes the rhythmic accompanying parts throughout; for reasons of playability, melodic lines are sometimes omitted.

* pronounced 'dye-ya'
† pronounced 'high-ya'

* pronounced 'high-ya'

good e - nough   if you be-lieve   that   hard must   be   right.____

ah   da   oh   ah   da   oh   ah____

ah   da   oh   ah   da   oh   ah____

ah   da   oh   ah   da   oh   ah____

dn   dn   doo   dn   dn   dn   dn   dn   doo   dn   dn   dn   dn   dn   doo

* pronounced 'high-ya'

Dedicated to Matt Jones.
Welcome home.

The Parting Glass

Trad. Scottish
arr. **SARAH QUARTEL**

Duration: 3 mins

A composer's note is available on the OUP website.

Also available in a version for TTBB unaccompanied (ISBN 978–0–19–352746–1).

done, a - las it was to__ none but me. And

all__ I've__ done for want__ of__ wit to mem - 'ry now I__

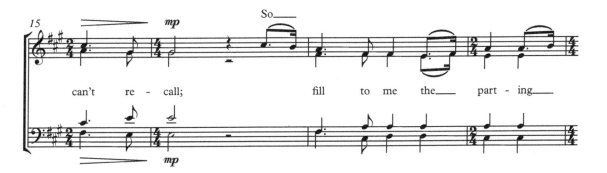

can't re - call; fill to me the__ part - ing__

glass, good_ night and joy be__ with you all.

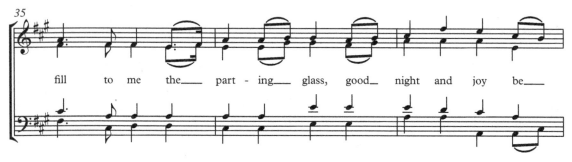

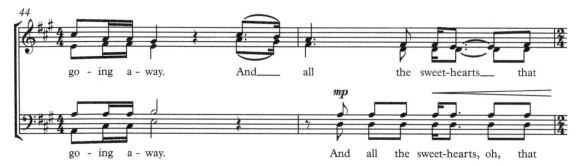